A Gift Book from Robert Frederick • The Kate Greenaway Collection

This edition © Robert Frederick Ltd.
Downwood, Claverton Down Road, Bath BA2 6DT

"The Kate Greenaway Collection"

First Published 1993
All rights reserved.

Acknowledgments:
Typesetting by Creative Design & Typesetting;
Reproduction in Hong Kong; Printing in the UK

Book of Games

Selections from the original,
written & illustrated by Kate Greenaway

SKIPPING

Two children each hold one end of a rope, and stand so that in turning it just touches the ground in the middle. How fast they turn entirely depends on the skipper. Two can skip at the same time over the rope if it is a fairly long one. In skipping singly it is more graceful to watch if the rope is thrown backwards over the head rather than forward under the feet.

PUSS IN THE CORNER

The child who represents puss stands in the middle, while the others stand at fixed stations round her. One then beckons to another saying: "Puss, puss, give me a drop of water!" when each runs and changes places. Puss then runs and tries to get into one of the places, if she succeeds, the one left out is puss.

TOPS

Tops are common enough objects to most people, but there is some skill required in spinning them. There are also many different games. For "Peg in the Ring" (played with a peg top), draw a circle about three feet in diameter. One player begins by throwing his top into the centre, and whilst it is spinning the other players peg their tops at it, but if it gets out of the ring, and ceases spinning, the owner may pick it up and peg it at any others spinning in the circle. To set whipping tops going, they should be rapidly twirled round with the hands, and whipped, not too hardly at first. An eel skin makes the best kind of whip. Races can be played with whip tops, the boy who can whip his top along at the greatest speed is the winner. Another game called "Encounters" consists in the players whipping their tops against each other till one of them falls.

TEAPOT

One player leaves the room, while the others decide on a word with many meanings. The absent player having been called in, his object is to find out the chosen word. To enable him to do this, the others converse about it, but instead of using the word itself, say "tea-pot" instead. For instance, if the word chosen be "rain," the players converse about it in the following manner: "We shall have 'tea-pot' (rain) tonight. When I was riding yesterday, the 'tea-pot' (rein) broke. The 'tea-pot' (reign) of Queen Victoria has been long and glorious." When the player correctly guesses the hidden word, the person whose remark enabled him to do so, leaves the room in his turn.

TWENTY QUESTIONS

One of the players is sent out of the room, and the others agree upon some subject, which he is to discover by asking twenty questions; and they must all be of such a nature as can be answered by "Yes" or "No."

WHAT IS MY THOUGHT LIKE?

One player thinks of some person or object and then asks each of the others in turn: "What is my thought like?" Each names some object and the leader then announces what his thought was; and each player is requested to prove the resemblance between his guess and the subject really chosen. If he cannot he must pay a forfeit.

HUNT THE RING

A ring is threaded on a long piece of string with the ends joined. The players stand in a circle, the cord passing through their closed hands. The ring circulates from one to another, while a player in the centre of the circle endeavours to find it. When he does so, the person in whose hand the ring is found takes his place.

SEE-SAW

A great deal of amusement may be derived from having a see-saw. It should be made of a thick plank of wood balanced over a fallen tree-trunk or other suitable erection. The players sit on the ends, balancing themselves as equally as possible, and go up and down. If one player will stand in the middle to work it, he can help to balance it and prevent a sudden jerk should anyone fall or get off without warning.

MARBLES

Many and various are the games which can be played with marbles. "Ring-taw" is a very favourite pastime. Two circles are drawn on the ground, the outer one six feet in diameter, the inner one nine inches. The players put one or more marbles inside the inner circle, and shoot one at a time from the outer ring at them. As long as a player does not send a marble out of the ring he may shoot indefinitely. When they have all fired once, they shoot from the place where their marbles remained, not the original starting place. If a player drives a marble out of the circle he wins it and shoots again, but if his "taw" remains in he is out, and must put a marble in the circle. There are other games called "Conqueror," "Increase Pound," "Three Holes," "Lag Out," and "Snops and Spans."

UP JENKINS

The company divide into two parties and sit round a table. One party then puts their hands under the table and a shilling or other small article is placed in one of the palms. The other side then calls out "Up Jenkins!" and the players whose side has the shilling concealed must all place their closed hands on the table. The opposite side must then guess in which hand the shilling is concealed. The hands that they think have not got it must be told to go down, but if one of those hands should contain it, the player must show it, and the same side hides the shilling again. But if all the hands but one are sent down without the shilling being found, then the player must give it up, and the opposite side hides it in the same manner.

TOUCH WOOD

All the children but one place themselves in various positions, each touching something that is wood. They keep constantly running from one wooden thing to another. The one left out runs after them, and the first she catches not touching wood takes her place.

BATTLEDORE & SHUTTLECOCK

This is a most convenient game, because one solitary individual can find amusement as well as any number, provided there is a bat for each player. The object of the game is to keep the shuttlecock going as long as possible.

HUNT THE SLIPPER

The children sit on the ground, or on low seats in a circle, with their knees raised. One has been left out; she brings a slipper, and giving it to one child says:

"Cobbler, cobbler, mend my shoe,
Get it done by half-past two."

She goes away, and comes back in about a minute and asks if it is done. (During this time the slipper has been passing round.)

The child answers, she thinks her neighbour has it; so the seeker passes on to her, and getting the same answer she has to go round till the slipper is found. If she is a long time finding it, the slipper may be thrown across the circle.

EARTH, AIR, FIRE & WATER

The players form a circle, and one stands in the centre holding a handkerchief knotted into a ball. He counts up to ten, then throws the ball into someone's lap, calling out either "Earth", "Air", "Fire", or "Water". If he cries "Earth", the person in whose lap the handkerchief has fallen must instantly name some animal which lives on the earth; if the word was "Water", some fish must be named; if "Fire", something that can exist in fire; if "Air", some bird. If he allows the ball-thrower to count up to ten without his answering he must pay a forfeit.

THE FEATHER GAME

The players sit close together, and one of them taking a piece of swansdown (or similar substance), blows it up into the air. The other players must keep it afloat by their breath; if anyone allows it to sink to the ground he must pay a forfeit.

MULBERRY BUSH

The children form into a ring, and holding hands
run round and sing:

> "Here we go round the mulberry bush,
> The mulberry bush, the mulberry bush;
> Here we go round the mulberry bush
> On a cold and frosty morning."

Then unloosening hands they pretend to wash them, and say:

> "This is the way we wash our hands,
> Wash our hands, wash our hands;
> This is the way we wash our hands
> On a cold and frosty morning."

They then go round in a ring again and sing "mulberry bush," to be again followed by pretending to wash faces, dresses, go to school, and anything they like.

THE STORY GAME

One of the players starts an original story, and leaves off in a very exciting place; his left-hand neighbour must instantly continue it, and also stops at an exciting place, when the thread of the story is resumed by the player on his left hand. For example, one player starts the following story: "One evening, several centuries ago, a knight was riding through a dark wood, when, hearing a noise, he looked up and saw—" Here the player stops, and his left-hand neighbour continues: "A band of robbers rapidly advancing towards him. He gave himself up for lost, when—" The story is continued by left-hand neighbour, and so the game goes on till the tale is finished by the last player.

TOM TIDDLER'S GROUND

One part of the field or lawn is marked off as Tom Tiddler's ground, over which Tom presides in solitary state. It is supposed to have a quantity of lumps of gold scattered about it. The other players venture on, and pretend to be picking up something, at the same time singing; "Here I am on Tom Tiddler's ground, picking up gold and silver!" He rushes after them, and if he succeeds in catching anybody, that one has to take his place as Tom Tiddler. Tom may not leave his own ground.

FOX & HEN

One of the players is chosen to be fox and another to be hen. All the others are chickens, and form a string at the back of the hen one behind another. They then advance to the fox's den and ask him the time. They repeat the question several times till he says it is twelve o'clock at night, when they must instantly run away as the fox will pursue them, the hen dodging the fox and trying to prevent his seizing the last chicken. When all the chickens have been captured the game is finished.

PROVERBS

One of the party is sent out of the room while the others choose a proverb. When one is selected each person in turn takes a word of the proverb which he must bring into his answer when questioned by the absent player, who asks a question of each in turn, and from their answers guesses the proverb.

HOP SCOTCH

Chalk out on the ground a figure like the accompanying diagram. Then the players "pink;" that is, throw their piece of tile, or lead, towards the pudding, or top of the figure. The one who lodges his tile there begins; if more than one succeeds in doing this, they "pink" again. The winner begins by standing at *, and throwing his tile onto the division marked 1; he then hops into the space and kicks the tile out to the starting point. Then he throws the tile into 2; hops into 1, then into 2, and kicks the tile out as before. He repeats this through the different numbers till he arrives at 8; here he may put his feet into 6 and 7 and rest himself, but he must begin hopping again before he kicks the tile home. He then goes on through 9, 10, 11, as before directed. 12 is another resting-place, where he may put down both feet. When he comes to plum pudding he must kick the tile with such force that it goes through all the other beds by one kick. In the other divisions it is not necessary to kick the tile so hard, as the player may hop as many times as he likes. If he throws the tile into a wrong number, or if it rests on a line, he loses his innings, whether kicking it out or throwing it in to begin with. He also misses his turn if he puts his feet down in what is not a resting-place, or if he puts his feet on a line, or kicks the tile outside the diagram.

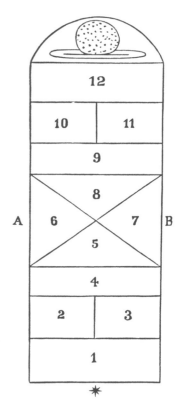

THE HAT GAME

A hat is placed on the ground, and the players (standing two or three paces from it) try to throw cards, one at a time, into it. This sounds much more easy to do than it really is.

ORANGES AND LEMONS

The two tallest players, taking the name of orange and lemon respectively, join hands, and holding them up form an arch under which the others pass in single file, holding on to each others' dresses, singing:

"Oranges and lemons," say the bells of St. Clements.
"Brickbats and tiles," say the bells of St. Giles.

"You owe me five farthings," say the bells of St Martin's.
"When will you pay me?" say the bells of Old Bailey.
"When I grow rich," say the bells of Shoreditch.
"When will that be?" say the bells of Stepney.
"I do not know," says the great bell of Bow.
Here comes a candle to light you to bed,
And here comes a chopper to chop off your head!

When the last one comes below the arms they descend and catch him, and he is asked in a whisper if he will be orange or lemon. He whispers the answer and joins whichever he has chosen holding on round her waist. The game continues thus till all are caught, when a tug-of-war ensues between the parties.

MUSICAL CHAIRS

Someone plays the piano. Chairs must be placed down the room, back to back, one less in number than the players who galop round them in time to the music. Suddenly it stops, and everybody then tries to get a chair, but as there is one short, someone will be left standing, and is then out of the game. A chair is taken away and the game goes on as before till only one player, the victor, is left.

HOOPS

Every child knows, or ought to know, the pleasure of bowling a hoop. What a nice ring there is about it, when on a fine frosty day the juvenile members of the family all turn out with hoops and race along the road. There is a very jolly game called "turnpikes," but it wants rather an open space; any number can play, only half the players need hoops. Two largish stones or bricks are placed side by side about six inches apart at regular intervals in a circle or along a road, each pair being guarded by a "pike-keeper." The bowlers, who all stand in a row, start at some little distance off and drive their hoops between the bricks. If they succeed in doing this, they steer round and go through again; but should anyone miss, he takes the place of the "pike-keeper" whose gate he missed and the "pike-keeper" becomes a bowler.

MAGIC MUSIC

The company sit in a circle, and one person is sent out of the room. Then the players either hide or alter something in the room or agree that the absent one shall do something, such as repeat a verse of poetry, etc. When they have decided the player is called in, and may ask whether it is something to find, alter, or do. He is told which it is, and someone must then begin playing on the piano. When he is near finding, altering or doing the thing decreed, the music is loud; but when he moves away from the thing hidden or altered, or does not guess what he has to do, the music is soft. It is by listening to its sound that the player is guided in performing his task.

HIDE-AND-SEEK

One child called "he" must hide his eyes at a place called "home", while the other children run and hide. When they are hidden they call whoop! Then "he," uncovering his eyes, runs out and tries to catch them before they can get "home." The one caught is "he" next time. If none are caught, then the same one must be "he" again.

SWINGS

A swing is the source of much innocent enjoyment which most children can have for a very small outlay. It consists of two upright posts, with a bar securely fastened horizontally; to this two ropes are tied to which a seat is attached. A bough of a tree is a more picturesque place for a swing, but trees are not always to be had for the wishing. Boat swings at fairs are irresistible attractions to most boys.

FROG IN THE MIDDLE

The child who represents the frog sits on a hassock in the
middle of the room, all the other children
run and dance round, singing:

"Frog in the middle, you can't catch me!
Frog in the middle, you can't catch me!"

"Frog" must try to catch them with her hands without getting up from her stool; the one who is caught has to take the place of "Frog."

RUSSIAN SCANDAL

The players sit in a circle and the leader whispers some anecdote or quotation to his left-hand neighbour, which he in turn repeats to the person next to him, and so the story is whispered round the circle, the last player relating aloud what has been told him. The original is then repeated, and it is amusing to see how entirely different the two narratives are.

THE ADJECTIVE GAME

One of the players leaves the room, while the others agree on an adjective which the absent player has to discover by questioning the others in turn. They must answer the questions in such a manner as will illustrate the adjective they have chosen. For instance, if they have fixed upon "abruptly," each player must answer the question put to him in an abrupt manner.

BLIND MAN'S BUFF

One child has her eyes blindfolded with a handkerchief so that she cannot see and is placed in the middle of the room. The children say to her: "How many horses has your father got?" She replies: "Three!" Children: "What colours are they?" She: "Black, White and Grey!"

Children: "Turn round three times and catch who you may!" They then turn her round three times, and she tries to catch anyone she can; the one caught has to be the next "blind man."

THE SHEPHERDESS AND THE WOLF

The players stand in a row at one end of the lawn while the shepherdess stands at the other. Half-way between the wolf must be concealed behind a bush. The shepherdess then calls out: "Sheep, sheep, come home!" One of the sheep replies: "I'm afraid of the wolf!" The shepherdess then says: "The wolf has gone to Devonshire and won't be home for seven years; sheep, sheep, come home!" The sheep then singly try to reach the shepherdess without being caught by the wolf. And so the game continues till all the players have either been caught by the wolf or reached the shepherdess safely.

THE HIDDEN WORD

One of the players leaves the room, while the others agree on a word. The absent player is then called in, and asks questions in turn of the others, who must all bring into their answers the word previously agreed upon. By this means the hidden word is guessed.

SOAP BUBBLES

Make a lather of soap and warm water, into which dip
a clay pipe; blow through it, a bubble
then issues from out the bowl —
a wonderful transparent globe,
glorious with iridescent
colours.

FOLLOW-MY-LEADER

An active and daring boy should be chosen as leader, the others follow him one behind the other, as closely as they can, doing as he does, and going where he goes, over gates, stiles and obstacles of all kinds. If anyone fails in accomplishing any one feat, he takes his place behind the rest. The next one who fails goes behind him, and so the game continues until the leader chooses to stop.

KITES

Most boys and girls know how to make and fly a kite. On a fine windy day, what can be more delightful than a good run over a common or breezy hill. Even a wet day need not come amiss; it gives a good opportunity for mending them or for making new ones. Japanese kites made in the shape of birds are amusing novelties and look very imposing. Paper "messengers" of all descriptions may be sent up the string; as they speed up, turning rapidly round and round, they can be followed by the eye till they reach the kite. Parachutes are also easily made, but as no string is attached, they are not so readily captured again.

TIRZA, OR DOUBLE TAGG

The players stand in pairs one behind another in the form of a circle facing the centre. There must be two odd players, one of whom runs away while the other catches. Directly the player who is being pursued places himself in front of any couple he is safe, while the hindermost person of the trio becomes the pursued. If he is caught before placing himself in front of another couple, he becomes the pursuer.

PROHIBITIONS

The players decide to dress a lady, but the following colours — green, yellow, blue and pink must not be used. One player asks of each in turn: "How will you dress my lady?" One says: "In a white silk dress!" Another: "With a wreath on her head!" and so on. Whoever mentions the forbidden colours pays a forfeit.

DOLLS

Most little girls like to possess a large family of dolls, though they may vary more in size and shape than an ancient Egyptian and a nineteenth century Master. There are the tiny little dolls which lie in uncomfortable attitudes in dolls' houses decked out in bright colours. There is the Dutch doll, with it stiffly-jointed legs and arms. There is the heavy old-fashioned wooden doll, as large as a good-sized baby. And now we have dolls which open and shut their eyes and say "Papa!" "Mamma!" Anyone who wishes to become a good needlewoman should try making dolls' clothes, where neat work is essential to the look of the thing.

BUZ

This is a very old game. All the players sit in a circle and begin to count in turn, but when the number 7, or any multiple of 7 cones, they say "buz" instead. If anyone forgets this, he is put out and the game commences over again. "Fiz" for five makes a variety.

SHADOW BUFF

A small sheet or table cloth must be fastened up at one end of the room. "Buff" sits facing it. A light is placed on a table a short distance behind "Buff," all the others in the room being extinguished. The players then pass in succession between "Buff" and the light, distorting their features and performing various odd antics, in order to make their shadows entirely different to their ordinary appearance. "Buff" must then guess whose shadow it is, when he guesses correctly, that player takes his place.

BALL

The game of ball is of very ancient origin, and there are many ways of amusing oneself with it. The players may stand in a ring a fair distance apart, and throw the ball from one to the other. Those who miss it have to remain in the attitude in which they were when they dropped the ball. At the end of the game the circle presents a very grotesque appearance. Another way is that whoever misses goes out of the game, so that the circle diminishes till only two remain; these continue till one fails and leaves the other the winner. A more exciting way is for the players to take the names of the days of the week, or, if more than seven, the months of the year. Then, for instance, Monday says; "The ball falls to Thursday." Thursday catches it and says; "The ball falls to Tuesday," and so on. Whoever misses pays a forfeit. Throwing the ball to the ground and letting it bounce before catching it, or making it bounce against a wall are other varieties of the game.

RUTH & JACOB

One person is blindfolded, and the rest dance in a circle round him till he points at some one. That person enters the ring, and the blindman calls out "Ruth"; "she" answers "Jacob"; and moving about within the circle so as to elude the blindman, continues to answer "Jacob" as often as the blindman calls out "Ruth." This continues until "Ruth" is caught. "Jacob" must then guess who it is he has caught; if he guesses correctly, "Ruth" takes his place, and the game goes on as before; if wrongly, the same one is "Jacob" again.

MARY'S GONE A-MILKING

All the children stand in a row, with joined hands, except one, who stands in front of them, and is Mother. They advance and retreat, singing:

"Mary's gone a-milking,
    a-milking, a-milking;
Mary's gone a-milking,
    dearest mother of mine!"

To which the Mother replies (advancing and retreating):

> "Take your pails and go after her, after her, after her;
>   Take your pails and go after her, dearest daughters of mine!"

Children: "Buy me a new pair of milking pails,
                milking pails, milking pails;
            Buy me a new pair of milking pails,
                dearest mother of mine!"

Mother: "What's your father to sleep in, sleep in, sleep in;
            What's your father to sleep in, dearest daughters of mine?"

Children: "Sleep in the washing-tub," &c
Mother: "What am I to wash in?," &c
Children: "Wash in a teacup," &c
Mother: "A teacup won't hold your father's shirt," &c
Children: "Wash in a thimble," &c
Mother: "A thimble won't hold the baby's cap," &c
Children: "Wash in the river," &c
Mother: "Suppose the clothes should float away," &c
Children: "Take a boat and go after them," &c
Mother: "Suppose the boat was to sink with me," &c
Children: "Then there'd be an end of you!" &c

Mother here rushes after the children. If she succeeds in catching one, that one must be Mother.

QUEEN ANNE AND HER MAIDS

One child covers her eyes, while the others, standing in a row close to each other, put their hands behind them. One has a ball concealed, which all pretend to have. They then call the one who has covered her eyes, and addressing her sing:

> "Queen Anne, Queen Anne, she sits in the sun;
>   As fair as a lily, as brown as a bun;
>   She sends you three letters, and begs you'll read one!"

To which Queen Anne replies:
>   "I cannot read one unless I read all,
>   So please Miss Mabel* deliver the ball."

If she has guessed correctly, the one who had the ball takes Queen Anne's place; but if it was a wrong one she hides her eyes again while the ball changes hands.

* Or whatever the name of the one she thinks has it is.

GENERAL POST

One person is selected as "postman" and blindfolded, the others all take the names of different places, except one, who is chosen as leader, and has a written list of the places chosen by the players. He then calls out: "The post is going from London to York," or any other names as the case may be. The persons named must then exchange seats, the "postman" trying to catch them as they move. Sometimes "general post" is called out, when all change their seats. Whoever is left out becomes "postman."